D1088165

# THE BILL OF RIGHTS
# EIGHTH AMENDMENT: THE RIGHT TO MERCY

## BY RICH SMITH

SERIES CONSULTANT: SCOTT HARR, J.D. CRIMINAL JUSTICE
DEPARTMENT CHAIR, CONCORDIA UNIVERSITY ST. PAUL

Published by ABDO Publishing Company, 8000 West 78th Street, Suite 310, Edina, MN 55439.
Copyright ©2008 by Abdo Consulting Group, Inc. International copyrights reserved in all countries.
No part of this book may be reproduced in any form without written permission from the publisher.
Abdo & Daughters™ is a trademark and logo of ABDO Publishing Company.

Printed in the United States.

**Editor:** John Hamilton
**Graphic Design:** Sue Hamilton
**Cover Design:** Neil Klinepier
**Cover Illustration:** Getty Images
**Interior Photos and Illustrations:** p 1 Constitution & flag, iStockphoto; p 5 prisoner behind bars, iStockphoto; p 7 victims burned at the stake, Corbis; p 9 prisoner with corrections officers, Getty Images; p 11 scales and skull, Corbis; p 12 death penalty protestors, AP Images; p 15 Texas death row, Corbis; pp 16-17 execution chamber, Getty Images; p 18 Thomas Edison and light bulb, AP Images; p 19 control panel and electric chair, AP Images; p 21 electric chair, AP Images; p 22 outside of gas chamber, AP Images; p 23 inside view of gas chamber, AP Images; p 24 Tombstone County Courthouse, iStockphoto; p 25 firing squad painting, Getty Images; p 26 money in hand, iStockphoto; p 27 bail bonds sign, iStockphoto; p 29 judge with gavel, Getty Images; p 32 U.S. Supreme Court building, iStockphoto.

Library of Congress Cataloging-in-Publication Data

Smith, Rich, 1954-
  Eighth Amendment : the right to mercy / Rich Smith.
    p. cm. -- (The Bill of Rights)
  Includes index.
  ISBN 978-1-59928-920-5
  1. Punishment--United States--Juvenile literature. 2. Capital punishment--United States--Juvenile literature. 3. United States. Constitution. 8th Amendment--Juvenile literature. I. Title.

KF9225.Z9S65 2008
345.73'077--dc22
                                    2007014578

# CONTENTS

# INTRODUCTION

The people of the United States have placed in the hands of government many powers. These include the power to protect the nation against invasion by enemy countries, the power to collect taxes, and the power to promote progress.

All these powers are good when the government uses them wisely. But sometimes government uses them in ways that are unjust and unfair. When that happens, the people become worried and fearful.

Of the many different powers granted by the American people to their government, the one that causes the most worry and fear is government's power to punish those who have been found guilty of crimes. Government can punish convicted criminals by making them pay money or by putting them in prison. In some cases, government can punish a criminal by ending that person's life.

No matter what form punishment takes, it is always a serious matter. That is why the Founding Fathers, the men who wrote the Bill of Rights into the Constitution of the United States, made sure to include an amendment guaranteeing that punishment must fit the crime. In other words, the government is not allowed to drop a piano on your head if you're found guilty of stealing a loaf of bread to feed your starving family. For stealing bread, a punishment that fits the crime might be to make you spend several weekends helping serve meals to the poor at a homeless shelter. But never would the punishment fit the crime of stealing bread if you were ordered to be killed.

The amendment that deals with punishment is the Eighth Amendment. Here is what it says: "Excessive bail shall not be required, nor excessive fines imposed, nor cruel and unusual punishments inflicted."

*Above:* The U.S. government can punish those who have been found guilty of crimes, but the Eighth Amendment states that no cruel and unusual punishment will be allowed.

# CRUEL AND UNUSUAL

In the summer of 1825, a South Carolina man was punished for a crime by being burned to death. That was the last time any convicted criminal in the United States received that form of punishment. The government stopped using burning because it was found to be a violation of the Eighth Amendment.

Burning was a punishment brought to the American colonies from England and elsewhere in Europe, where it was common. Some other forms of punishment used in Europe were also used in the colonies, but only for a short time because they were so horrible. For example, there was the punishment of pressing. This was where a criminal was made to lie flat on his back while heavy slabs of granite stone were built up on top of his chest. The English also had a punishment called drawing and quartering. It involved cutting open the prisoner's belly and removing his intestines, then setting them on fire while he was forced to watch. After that, his head was chopped off and his body sliced into four parts.

These punishments may seem cruel beyond belief to you. They are the kind of thing the Eighth Amendment made sure would never be permitted in the United States. But many forms of punishment are nowhere near as bad as those we've already mentioned. For instance, punishing someone by taking away his or her United States citizenship is nothing at all like drawing and quartering. Yet taking away citizenship as punishment is also forbidden under the Eighth Amendment. The U.S. Supreme Court said so in its 1958 ruling in the case of *Trop v. Dulles*.

For a punishment to be unconstitutional, it must be cruel and unusual. But what makes a punishment cruel and unusual? In 1972 the U.S. Supreme Court came up with a list. First, the punishment had to violate the human dignity of the person receiving the punishment. Second, the punishment had to be one that was not handed out equally or in a consistent way.

*Above:* A painting by Paolo Uccello of victims being burned at the stake. In 1825, a South Carolina man was the last criminal in the U.S. to be punished by being burned to death. The Eighth Amendment determined that this was a cruel and unusual form of punishment.

Third, the punishment had to be something that most people would find sickening even to think about. Fourth, the punishment had to be unnecessary for the type of crime involved.

The Supreme Court on other occasions ruled that a punishment is unconstitutional only if it is both cruel *and* unusual. So a punishment might meet the definition of cruel but still be lawful if it is usual or common. And a punishment might be unusual but still be OK because hardly anybody considers it cruel.

# THE THREE-STRIKES RULE FOR HABITUAL OFFENDERS

SOME CRIMINALS KEEP getting in serious trouble, over and over again. Many states today sentence these people to prison for extremely long times. Usually, this happens if a person has a record of three separate convictions for felony crimes. It is formally known as *mandatory sentencing for habitual offenders*. It is also more popularly known as "three strikes and you're out."

In three-strikes states, the penalty for being found guilty of that third felony can be life imprisonment. This extremely harsh sentence accomplishes two things: First, it gets hardened criminals off the streets. Second, it provides what is called a *deterrent effect*. That means it discourages people from committing illegal acts. In this case, people with two strikes already against them will be motivated to stay on the right side of the law.

But not everyone is motivated in that way. Some critics of three strikes believe that the only motivation the repeat offender has is to not be convicted the third time. For example, they argue that a two-time ex-convict will be motivated to kill any witnesses to his latest crime in order to reduce the odds of being caught and convicted again. Also, the critics say that this same person will be more willing to shoot it out with police in hopes of escaping arrest rather than surrender peacefully and face what could be a life sentence no matter what.

Three-strikes states usually set up their systems so that the only criminals affected are those with prior convictions for truly serious or violent felonies. But this has led to situations that make three strikes seem like an unconstitutional form of punishment.

For example, in California, three strikes requires that the minor crime of shoplifting be called a felony if the accused was previously convicted for robbery, burglary, or some other type of theft that actually is a felony. That's how a former California felon by the name of Leandro Andrade ended up back in prison for life. His third felony? He shoplifted some movies from a video store.

Another criminal who made headlines in California with a three-strikes life sentence had done nothing more than steal a set of golf clubs. Still another was imprisoned for life because he swiped a slice of pizza. And there was one who lost his freedom over the theft of four chocolate chip cookies.

These and similar cases led to court challenges of three strikes. The first to reach the U.S. Supreme Court was *Ewing v. California* (2003). This case was brought by the man who stole the golf clubs. The High Court's decision disappointed those who wanted three strikes ruled unconstitutional. The justices found that three strikes might seem cruel but is not unusual as they understood the Eighth Amendment to mean. Therefore, three strikes was an OK form of punishment, the Supreme Court decided.

*Above:* A man is led away by corrections officers. In three-strikes states, someone who is found guilty of three crimes can be sentenced to life in prison. Some believe that this harsh penalty gets hardened criminals off the streets, while others say it's cruel.

# THE ULTIMATE PUNISHMENT

Sometimes crimes are so horrible that nothing less than the worst possible punishment allowed under the Eighth Amendment will let people feel as if justice was served. However, not everyone agrees on what is the worst possible punishment for the worst possible crimes. Take murder, for example. Most people can agree it is a truly terrible crime. But many of those same people believe that the only proper punishment for it is death. On the other hand, many do not believe death is a proper punishment. They believe instead that the murderer should be locked away in prison for the rest of his or her life and never be allowed to go free.

The courts in America have long accepted that death is a punishment permitted by the Eighth Amendment. But murder is just one of several very serious crimes that can be punished that way. Other such crimes include treason and spying for an enemy country, really bad kinds of kidnappings and rapes, hijacking an airplane, causing a train wreck that ends up killing someone, telling a lie under oath that ends up getting someone killed, and being a big-time drug lord. All of these are officially known as *capital offenses*. However, these days, the death penalty is usually given only to convicted murderers.

Another term for the death penalty is *capital punishment*. Capital punishment is handed out by the federal government for convictions in cases where federal capital offenses have been committed. Capital punishment is also handed out in 38 states for convictions in cases where state capital offenses have been committed.

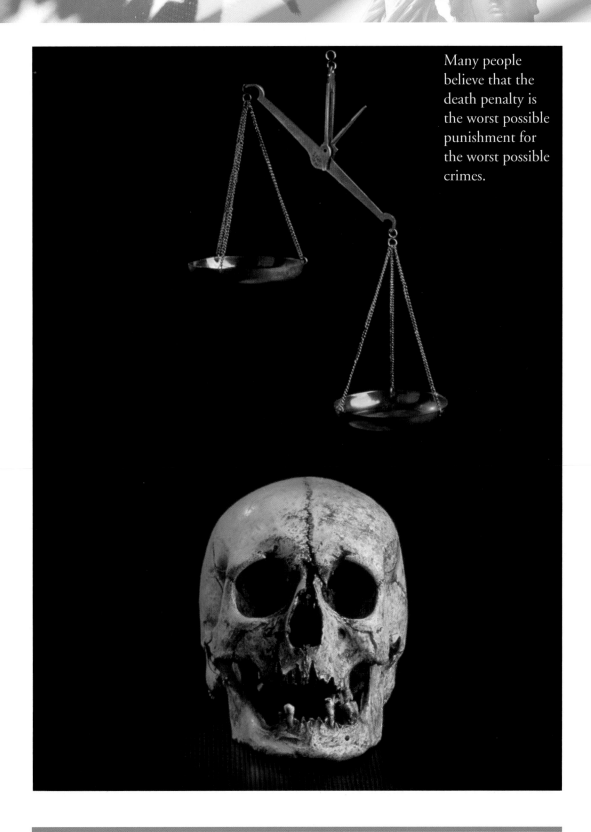

Many people believe that the death penalty is the worst possible punishment for the worst possible crimes.

*Above:* Some people believe that capital punishment is wrong. They believe that the death penalty should be stopped and murderers should instead face life in prison.

There was a period of four years when the death penalty was declared unconstitutional at the federal level and in the states. This began in 1972 when the U.S. Supreme Court issued a famous ruling in the case of *Furman v. Georgia*. William Henry Furman was a burglar who sometimes carried a loaded handgun with him on his heists. One day, as he was stealing from a home, the people who lived there caught him red-handed. Furman was startled and made a dash for the door. But he stumbled and fell. When he landed on the floor, the gun he'd brought with him went off by itself. The bullet struck and killed one of the people. Police later arrested Furman, who confessed in writing to the crime. He was tried, found guilty, and sentenced to death. His attorney then appealed the death sentence. The appeal worked its way to the Supreme Court, which found that the death penalty was a cruel and unusual punishment. It based that finding on the fact that every state had its own different way of deciding who would get the death penalty. The justices of the High Court said that the American system of handing out capital punishment was very uneven and unfair.

The Furman decision made opponents of the death penalty very happy. It is their belief that capital punishment is wrong. They believe society stoops to the level of the murderers it condemns when it executes them. But there were also many people who were angry about the Furman decision. These death penalty proponents believe that capital punishment makes people who might be tempted to commit murder think twice about doing it. Also, they believe that putting a murderer to death guarantees that he or she will never leave prison and murder again.

The death penalty became once more constitutional in 1976 when the Supreme Court upheld new laws put in place by the states to make death sentences fair and more uniform. Since then, however, the Supreme Court placed a few limits on the death penalty. For example, its ruling in *Atkins v. Virginia* (2002) made clear that there can be no executions of the mentally disabled. And the High Court's decision in *Roper v. Simmons* (2005) outlawed capital punishment for people who are younger than 18 at the time they commit a crime.

# DEATH BY INJECTION

M ore than 1,000 convicted criminals were put to death in the U.S. between 1976 and 2006. That's an average of about 33 or 34 executions during each of those 30 years. However, there were many times that number of convicted criminals who were supposed to be executed but were spared instead. A few had their death sentences lifted by a pardon from the governor of their state. Most of the others were moved off of "death row" when their sentences were thrown out on appeal. As many as two-thirds of all death sentences in the United States are reversed because of some technicality, such as the failure to give the accused person his full due-process rights.

*Facing Page:* A death-row inmate in Texas stands before the prison doors. Nationwide, many death-row criminals have had their sentences reversed, but on average, more than 30 executions happen each year. Since 1976, the state of Texas has had the most number of prisoners executed. Since January 2007, the state of California has the most number of prisoners on death row.

Today, in the early part of the 21$^{st}$ century, there are five constitutionally permitted ways of putting a condemned criminal to death. The most widely used is lethal injection, which involves pumping deadly amounts of drugs into the condemned person's body. This is a medical-type procedure, but it is rare that a doctor or nurse will perform it. Medical professionals feel it is their job to save lives, not end them. Instead, a non-medical person who has been trained to administer lethal injections sets up the equipment and injects the drugs.

The equipment includes a table similar to what you would find in your family doctor's office, and also an infusion pump machine. The machine is on a metal stand that has a tall pole with a hooked end to hold three clear plastic bags of liquid drugs. The table has straps to tie down the condemned criminal's arms and legs. That is so he cannot struggle to get off the table once the execution begins.

After the condemned criminal is strapped down, thin plastic tubes with needle ends are poked into the veins of his or her arm. The other end of the tubes connect to the infusion pump machine, which pulls the lethal drugs from the overhanging bags into the condemned's arm.

The procedure takes place at the prison in a room specially designed for lethal injection executions. The room is usually inside a small auditorium. The room has large glass windows so that people in the auditorium can look in and witness the execution. People who witness executions are invited by the prison warden. Invited witnesses might include news reporters and important civic leaders, along with the condemned criminal's nearest relatives, closest friends from outside the prison, his or her attorneys, and a pastor or priest. Sometimes the invited witnesses include family members of the crime victim instead of family members of the condemned criminal. In some places, only the prison staff is allowed to witness the execution.

The execution room itself is usually divided into two parts. The person to be put to death is in one part. The infusion pump and the lethal drugs are in another. The two parts may be separated by a curtain or by a solid wall with small ports for the tubes to pass through.

Three different types of drugs are loaded into the infusion pump. The first one to reach the condemned criminal is meant to put him into the deepest possible sleep. The next one causes his breathing to stop. The final drug makes his heart quit beating. It takes about seven minutes for all the drugs to be pumped into him and for death to occur.

Lethal injection is said to be the kindest, gentlest way there is for executing criminals. But people who oppose capital punishment say this method of ending life could be cruel and unusual if the first drug given to the condemned criminal were to wear off or not take effect before the other drugs begin working.

*Right:* The execution chamber in the federal prison in Terre Haute, Indiana. A condemned prisoner is strapped onto the table and given a mixture of drugs that cause his or her breathing and heart to stop.

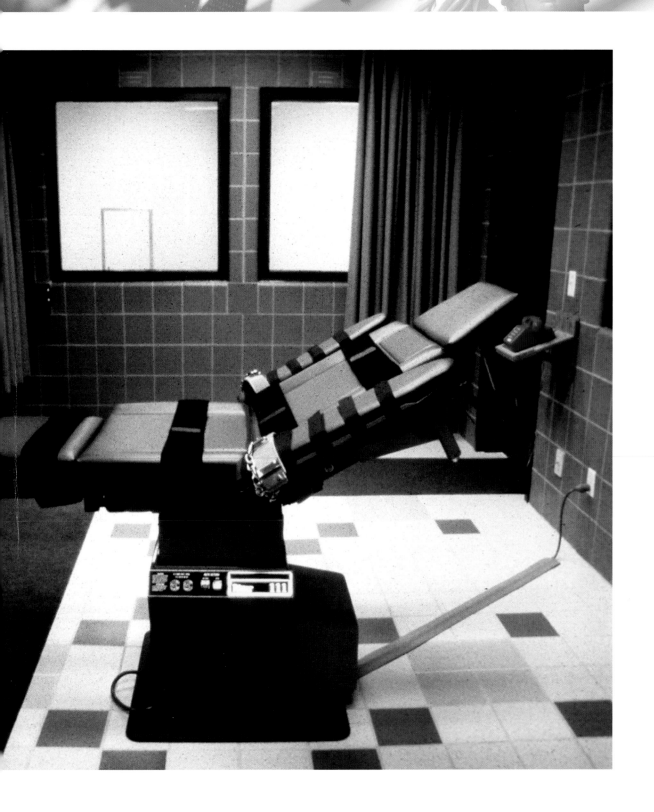

# THE ELECTRIC CHAIR

The first thing many Americans think of when they hear the words "death penalty" is a murderer being executed in an electrified chair. However, the electric chair isn't used in many states any more. In the first half of the 20th century it was the most common way to take the life of a condemned man or woman. In old-time gangster movies, they referred to it as "the chair." In newspapers of that era, they sometimes gave it the nickname Old Sparky.

The way a person is executed using an electric chair is by sending enough high-voltage current through his body to short-circuit his heart, lungs, and brain, which causes these organs to completely stop working.

The setup for an execution by electric chair is much the same as it is for a lethal injection. The chair is inside a special room within a small auditorium of the prison. The chair is big and boxy. It has straps to tie down the prisoner. When it is time for the execution to take place, the prisoner is brought into the room and seated in the chair. His legs and head are shaved bald. On top of his head is placed a metal cap, and on his legs a metal clamp. The cap and clamp each have heavy-duty electrical cables connected to them. The cables are attached to a switch. The condemned criminal is killed when the switch is turned to the "on" position and the electricity flows through the cables. So much electricity is drawn through the cables that it causes the lights in the auditorium to grow dim or flicker.

The electricity is delivered in two or more jolts of about 2,000 volts each. That's over 15 times more powerful than the electricity that comes out of the wall socket at your home.

*Below:* Thomas Edison, the man who invented the light bulb, also helped create the first electric chair.

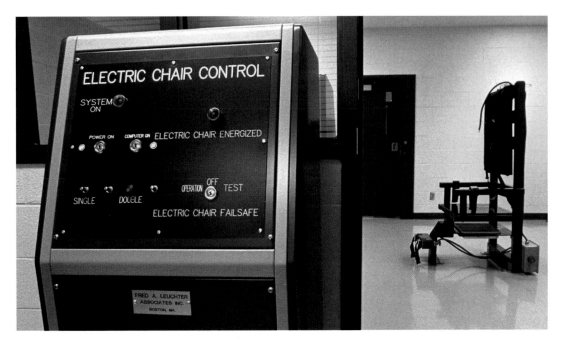

The first 2,000-volt jolt is meant to cause the prisoner to instantly pass out so that he does not feel the pain of what will follow. The next jolts are what bring death. The executioner keeps the electricity flowing long enough to guarantee that the condemned criminal will be dead by the time it is turned off.

The first electric chair execution took place in the year 1890. The idea for this method of court-ordered death came from a dentist who had seen a workman accidentally electrocuted after falling into a power generator. In fact, the word "electrocution" was invented by combining the words "electricity" and "execution." Electrocution originally meant death by electric chair. Years later, electrocution came to be the word everybody uses mainly to mean accidental death from contact with electricity.

The dentist took his idea for the electric chair to Thomas Edison, the man who invented the light bulb, the movie camera, the sound recorder, and many other important things. Edison thought the electric chair might be a very humane way to execute condemned criminals. So he assigned to one of his helpers the job of building the first electric chair.

*Above:* The control panel and electric chair in a Nashville, Tennessee, prison. Originally, the word "electrocution" meant death by electric chair.

Forty years later, more than half of the states in the U.S. were using electric chairs. But most of them stopped approximately 40 years after that. They got rid of their electric chairs because that form of execution had by then come to be widely seen as cruel. Sometimes a condemned criminal did not die immediately after the switch was thrown and had to be given extra jolts of electricity to finish him off. There were also times when the criminal died quickly but not before his body exploded in flames. All of these things had been observed by horrified witnesses, who were present to make sure the executions were properly conducted.

One of the worst of these executions-gone-wrong happened in 1946 when Louisiana attempted to end the life of a 17-year-old drugstore helper who had murdered his boss. The young man's name was Willie Francis. Witnesses at the execution heard him cry out in pain and beg for the electricity to be turned off, which caused the execution to be stopped. Francis immediately sued the state to prevent the government from trying again to put him to death. His attorney claimed that any attempt to re-execute Francis would be a cruel and unusual punishment because nobody is ever executed twice. The attorney also argued that trying to re-execute Francis would be a violation of the prisoner's Fifth Amendment right to not face double jeopardy. The case went all the way to the U.S. Supreme Court. In 1947, the High Court ruled in *State of Louisiana Ex Rel. Francis v. Resweber* that Francis could be taken back to the electric chair and it would not be a violation of his rights under either the Eighth or Fifth Amendments. Francis was put to death later that same year.

As of the early part of the 21st century, Nebraska is the last state to still have the electric chair as its only official way of executing condemned prisoners. Other states where it is available as a backup method of execution include Alabama, Florida, Illinois, Oklahoma, South Carolina, and Virginia.

*Facing Page:* An electric chair used by the Greensville Correctional Center in Jarratt, Virginia. A common nickname of the electric chair is Old Sparky. In the first half of the 20th century, death by electrocution was the most common way to take the life of a condemned prisoner.

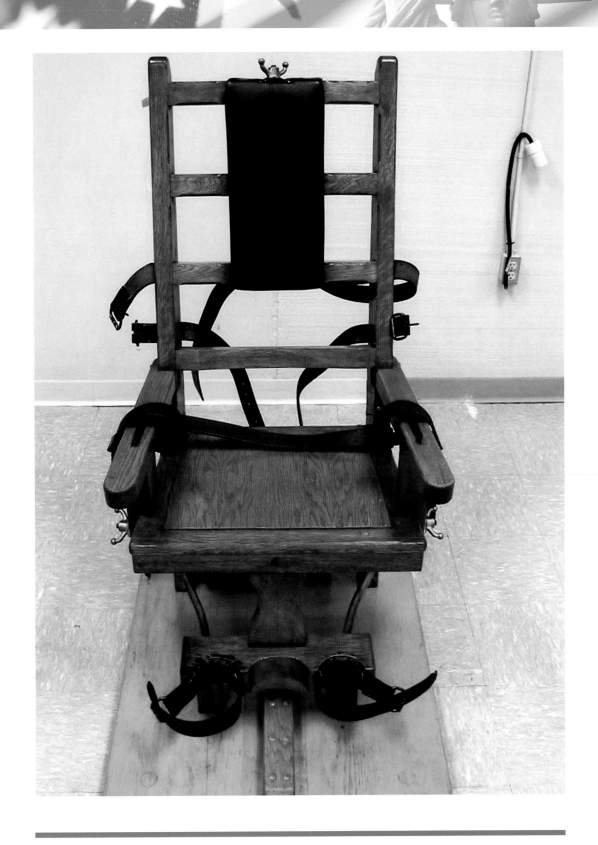

# THE GAS CHAMBER

A number of the states that stopped using the electric chair switched to a method of execution they hoped people would accept as more humane. That method was the gas chamber. It was first used in the 1920s.

A gas chamber is like the room where lethal injections and electrocutions take place. It is located in a small auditorium where witnesses can view the proceedings. Inside the room is a chair with straps to hold the condemned prisoner and prevent him from struggling free once the execution begins. The big difference with this room is that it is airtight. That means it has special seals on the doors and around the windows to make sure none of the air inside the room can seep out into the auditorium. That's very important because the condemned criminal is executed by filling the room with a deadly poisonous gas called hydrogen cyanide.

The first step in executing someone in a gas chamber involves loading potassium cyanide pellets into a container underneath the chair where the condemned criminal sits. The container has two separate sections inside it. The top section holds the potassium cyanide pellets. The bottom section holds sulfuric acid that will be poured in after the prisoner is seated. When the moment to begin the execution arrives, a lever is pulled from outside the sealed chamber. This causes the potassium cyanide pellets in the top section of the container to drop into the bottom section, where they mix with the sulfuric acid. The two chemicals coming into contact with one another produce a toxic cloud of hydrogen cyanide that fills the entire room. The prisoner passes out quickly and does not feel a thing if he inhales the fumes deeply. The gas will do the rest in less than a minute.

*Below:* A 1990 photo of the outside of the gas chamber in San Quentin State Prison, San Francisco, California.

*Above:* The inside of San Quentin State Prison's gas chamber. A condemned prisoner is strapped into the chair and sealed inside the room. A deadly gas called hydrogen cyanide fills the room and ends the prisoner's life.

We the People
of the United States, in order to form a more perfect...
...insure domestic Tranquility, provide for the common defence, promote the general Welfare, and secure the Blessings of...

*Above:* A gallows at the Tombstone County Courthouse in Tombstone, Arizona. Although now a historical site, five criminals were executed here in 1884, and two more in 1900. Death by hanging is still legally allowed in the United States.

Unfortunately, most condemned criminals don't inhale deeply when they see the cloud forming. Instead, they try holding their breath for as long as they can. People who think the gas chamber is a cruel form of punishment say that prisoners suffer a slower death when they hold their breath. And sometimes prisoners who do inhale deeply don't pass out right away. As a result, they die in pain. Plus, the gas chamber reminds too many people of how the Nazis put more than 6 million people to death in concentration camps during World War II. All these problems convinced most of the states that used the gas chamber to change to the lethal injection method. However, several states kept their gas chambers as backups.

There are two other forms of execution legally allowed in the United States. One is death by hanging. The other is death by firing squad.

*Above:* A painting of a firing squad preparing to execute prisoners. In the United States, death by firing squad is one of several forms of execution allowed. The other forms include lethal injection, the gas chamber, electrocution, and hanging. Most states today use lethal injection as their main method of capital punishment.

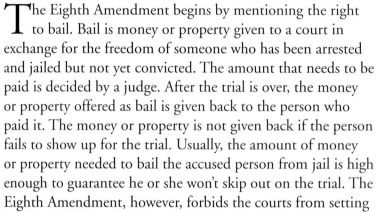

# THE RIGHT TO BAIL

The Eighth Amendment begins by mentioning the right to bail. Bail is money or property given to a court in exchange for the freedom of someone who has been arrested and jailed but not yet convicted. The amount that needs to be paid is decided by a judge. After the trial is over, the money or property offered as bail is given back to the person who paid it. The money or property is not given back if the person fails to show up for the trial. Usually, the amount of money or property needed to bail the accused person from jail is high enough to guarantee he or she won't skip out on the trial. The Eighth Amendment, however, forbids the courts from setting the amount of money or property needed for bail at too high a sum. The same is true of fines that a court might order a convicted criminal to pay as part or all of his punishment.

*Below:* People who have been arrested and are awaiting trial may get out of jail temporarily by posting bail— money they pay to ensure they will return for trial.

Setting bail and fines too high was a trick sometimes used by courts before the United States became a country. Prisoners that the government wanted locked away could be kept in jail for very long times. It was a clever trick because the government could claim it wasn't at fault if the accused person couldn't "make bail" or pay the fine. And by shifting the blame in that manner, the government was able to chill any anger people might otherwise have felt toward the government for unjustly imprisoning someone.

*Left:* Many businesses that provide bail bonds are open day and night to allow arrested people the chance to post bail.

Today, each state has its own rules about bail. Usually, though, an accused person is automatically entitled to bail unless the crime is very serious, or unless there is strong evidence that the person will run away and disappear.

Sometimes a person can walk from jail without having to put up any money or property. This is called being *released on one's own recognizance*. What that means is the accused does nothing more than promise to appear in court on the date set for his or her trial. The promise is considered to be as good as gold. But if the accused fails to appear, the judge will issue an order to collect the money or property that normally would have been set as bail.

It is common in America for bail to be paid through someone hired by the accused or by his or her family or friends. Such a person is known as a *bail bondsman*. Here is how it works: Say you are arrested for a crime and the judge sets your bail at $50,000. That's a lot of money to come up with on your own. So you turn to a bail bondsman. She has the $50,000 you need. She agrees to go to the courthouse on your behalf and give the clerk $50,000 if you promise to pay her 10 percent of the bail total, which equals $5,000. It's still a lot of money for you to pay, but not as bad as raising the whole bail amount yourself.

# CONCLUSION

The Eighth Amendment in the Bill of Rights applies to the states as well as the federal government. Amendments that apply at both the state and federal levels are called *incorporated amendments.*

The Eighth Amendment, like the other nine amendments that make up the Bill of Rights, limits the ability of government to interfere with the freedoms enjoyed by Americans. Many mistakenly think the Bill of Rights represents the government giving liberties to the American people. In reality, the Bill of Rights represents the American people restricting the power of their government. That is a very important idea to understand. What it means is that America is a land where the people are the rulers and the government is the servant. In most other places around the world the exact opposite is the case: the government rules and the people are servants.

Many Americans believe that the Eighth Amendment to the Constitution is one big reason why so many foreign people want to come and live in the United States. It is an amendment that shows Americans believe in mercy. We entrust to our government the most fearsome power of all, the power to end the life of a fellow human. Because we value mercy so highly, the power to take away that life is a power the government uses only rarely and not with any eagerness.

*Above:* While the United States prides itself on its ability to seek justice and punish wrongdoers, the Eighth Amendment helps define the American people's right to mercy.

# GLOSSARY

## AMENDMENT

When it was created, the Constitution wasn't perfect. The Founding Fathers wisely added a special section. It allowed the Constitution to be changed by future generations. This makes the Constitution flexible. It is able to bend to the will of the people it governs. Changes to the Constitution are called amendments. The first 10 amendments are called the Bill of Rights. An amendment must be approved by two-thirds of both houses of Congress. Once that happens, the amendment must be approved by three-fourths of the states. Then it becomes law. This is a very difficult thing to do. The framers of the Constitution didn't want it changed unless there was a good reason. There have been over 9,000 amendments proposed. Only 27 of them have been ratified, or made into law. Some amendments changed the way our government works. The Twelfth Amendment changed the way we elect our president. The Twenty-Second Amendment limits a president to two terms in office. Constitutional amendments have also increased the freedoms of our citizens. The Thirteenth Amendment finally got rid of slavery. And the Nineteenth Amendment gave women the right to vote.

## BILL OF RIGHTS

The first 10 amendments to the United States Constitution make up what is known as the Bill of Rights. The Bill of Rights lists the special freedoms every human is born with and is able to enjoy in America. Also, the Bill of Rights tells the government that it cannot stop people from fully using and enjoying those freedoms unless the government has an extremely good reason for doing so.

## DOUBLE JEOPARDY

The act of putting a person on trial more than once for the same crime. The Fifth Amendment to the United States Constitution specifically forbids this.

## DUE PROCESS

Fair treatment through the judicial system. Due process protects Americans by making sure that government behaves in a fair and honorable way when it tries to put a person in prison or take away his or her property. There are two types of due process. One is procedural due process. The other is substantive due process. Procedural due process is about the rules or procedures the government must follow when taking action against someone.

Substantive due process is about making sure the government does not have one set of rules when it acts against someone and then a different set when dealing with another person. Substantive due process means the rules government follows must work the exact same for one person as they do for everyone else.

## Felony

A crime such as murder, rape, or burglary, that often involves violence. A felony is a serious crime that is usually punishable by imprisonment for more than one year or by death.

## Founding Fathers

The men who participated in the Constitutional Convention in 1787, especially the ones who signed the Constitution. Some of the Founding Fathers included George Washington, Benjamin Franklin, John Rutledge, Gouverneur Morris, Alexander Hamilton, and James Madison.

## High Court

Another name for the United States Supreme Court.

## Sue

To bring a lawsuit against a person or institution in a court of law.

## Supreme Court

The United States Supreme Court is the highest court in the country. There are nine judges on the Supreme Court. They make sure local, state, and federal governments are following the rules spelled out in the United States Constitution. Our understanding of the Constitution evolves over time. It is up to the Supreme Court to decide how the Constitution is applied to today's society. When the Supreme Court rules on a case, other courts in the country must follow the decision in similar situations. In this way, the laws of the Constitution are applied equally to all Americans.

## World War II

A war that was fought from 1939 to 1945, involving countries around the world. The United States entered the war after Japan's bombing of the American naval base at Pearl Harbor, in Oahu, Hawaii, on December 7, 1941.

# INDEX

The U.S. Supreme Court building in Washington, D.C.